Good Feeding Guide

Baby Tips™
The Little Terror

D0424397

Other books in the Baby Tips™ series
by Charlotte Preston and Trevor Dunton

∽

The Little Terror: Good Sleeping Guide
The Little Terror: Good Behavior Guide
The Little Terror: First Six Weeks

Good Feeding Guide

Baby Tips™
The Little Terror

CHARLOTTE PRESTON, RN   TREVOR DUNTON

FISHER BOOKS

⌣ For Alfie, Sophie, Tilly, Theo, Emilio and Sofia ∿

Publishers: Howard W. Fisher, Helen V. Fisher

Managing Editor: Sarah Trotta

North American Editor: Melanie Mallon

Book Production: Randy Schultz

Illustrations: Trevor Dunton

Cover Design: Randy Schultz

Published by Fisher Books, LLC
5225 W. Massingale Road
Tucson, Arizona 85743
(520) 744-6110

Printed in U.S.A.
Printing 5 4 3 2 1

Library of Congress Cataloging-in-Publication Data
Preston, Charlotte, 1935-
    The little terror good feeding guide / Charlotte
        Preston, Trevor Dunton. — North American ed.
        p. cm. — (Baby tips for new moms and dads)
    "First published in Great Britain in 1998 by Metro
        Books"—Copr. p.
    ISBN 1-55561-200-8
    1. Infants—Nutrition Humor. 2. Child rearing humor.
    3. Infants—Care Humor. I. Dunton, Trevor. II. Title.
    III. Title: Good Feeding Guide. IV. Series.
RJ216.P685 1999
613.2'083'2—dc21   99-36707
                                              CIP

First published in Great Britain in 1998 by Metro Books, an imprint of Metro Publishing Limited,
19 Gerrard Street, London W1V 7LA

North American edition © 1999 Fisher Books, LLC
Text © 1998, 1999 Charlotte Preston and Trevor Dunton
Illustrations © 1998, 1999 Trevor Dunton

Notice: The information in this book is true and complete to the best of our knowledge. It is offered with no
guarantees on the part of the authors or Fisher Books. Authors and publisher disclaim all liability with use of
this book.

An extra note for parents with girls:
You'll find that throughout the Little Terror books we refer to babies as "he."
Please don't think we've neglected your daughters! It's purely in the interests of clarity and space.
Using he/she, him/her, himself/herself is cumbersome to read and uses valuable space that we wanted to
devote to more useful topics. So, please read "she" for "he."

CONTENTS

SOLIDS, HERE WE COME!

This book is about introducing your Little Terror (LT) to the joys of solid food and making this change in his diet as smooth and problem-free as possible. You'll learn how to help LT form good habits, so he likes the foods that are best for his health and development. We'll explain why certain foods are better than others and offer simple, practical ways to deal with

eating problems. This book is also about making mealtimes enjoyable. You're going to have plenty of them, so have fun.

Until now, the decisions about LT's diet have been easy. The breast- or formula milk he's been guzzling for the last 4 months has had all the right stuff in it to help him develop into the strong, healthy, gurgling Little Terror he is now.

When your baby starts eating "real" food, it's an exciting time, but also one that raises a lot of questions. What do you give LT to eat? When do you start? Will he like it? You'll probably be overwhelmed by advice from friends, relatives, people you just met, magazines, radio and TV. Babies from different cultures eat all different kinds of weaning foods even though, physically, they are the same. This book will help you make your own choices.

WEANING

Since you're reading this, you're probably getting ready to introduce LT to the wonders of solid food. He'll love exploring different flavors and textures, discovering what happens when he tries to eat too much, learning how to bite and chew and figuring out what to do with his tongue. Eventually, he'll even get the hang of a cup and a spoon.

No one likes waiting forever to eat, so be ready for him to scream with frustration because he can't eat quickly enough. His tears can be upsetting at first, but it won't be long before he realizes that sharing mealtimes with you can be fun.

His food doesn't have to be complicated. In many countries, weaning simply means giving a mashed-up version of what the rest of the family is eating.

Start feeding him some solids after 4 months. If your baby was born early, you'll need to delay solids until the time he would have been 4 months old, if he hadn't been in such a hurry to be born.

Signs that he's ready to start eating solids

❀ He gets excited when you're eating and looks expectantly at the food on your plate.

❀ He feeds more often and doesn't seem as satisfied.

❀ He is 4 months old (or, if he was premature, when he *would have been* 4 months old, if he hadn't been born early).

What should you give him?

When you introduce LT to solids, you're setting up his eating habits for life. Research has shown that babies are far more open to new tastes and flavors than was previously thought, and 4 to 5 months is when they are most receptive. Babies have a natural curiosity and love of adventure, but if you feed him only bland foods, LT will only want to eat bland foods.

So, adapt what you're having (see pages 25-26 for exceptions) and start introducing different tastes from the beginning.

Stage 1
4 to 6 Months

Get ready

Basic weaning kit

- ❀ plastic bibs
- ❀ high chair
- ❀ sterilizer

- ❀ small electric blender
- ❀ bowls and spoons
- ❀ trainer cup for later

Sterilize all of his utensils every day and wash them in hot, soapy water between uses. Sterilize bottles, nipples and pacifiers too. To keep germs away, always wash your hands before preparing LT's food.

Get set

Don't wear designer clothes at mealtimes. It's going to be messy. Have his bib handy and prepare the food before giving him his milk. Also keep a towel nearby to wash him afterward.

Go!

So today's the day. Choose a time after a midday feeding. The goal at first is to get him to eat solids from a spoon, not to satisfy hunger. Once he has mastered the art, offer food when he is hungrier.

Offer a little purée—warm, not hot—on the tip of a clean plastic spoon, or even on your finger. . .

Don't force him. If he refuses his food, leave it and try again tomorrow.

Mealtimes are great for getting to know each other. Talk to him in funny voices. Tell him what a good boy he is. Make eye contact between mouthfuls.

Join in with a glass of iced tea or a snack (you don't have to spill it all over yourself, though), and he'll learn that mealtimes are special, something you do together. Try to relax and enjoy it.

What to give (all foods must be puréed)

Read through the list below. At first, breast or formula milk is still the main food, with solids as extra. But, after a few weeks, the nourishment LT gets from solids will increase, and gradually he'll drink less milk. By 6 months he could be eating two or three meals a day, having breast or formula milk before or after meals.

Do give

❀ Your own foods puréed, such as fruits and vegetables: bananas, apples, carrots, pears, spinach, potatoes, sweet potatoes, avocados and many others (if you purée a lot of fruit or vegetables, you can freeze most of it in ice-cube trays and give LT one cube a day, thawed and warmed up)

❀ Thin cooked cereal made from rice or corn

❀ Commercial baby foods, such as rice cereal and first baby foods, when you're in a hurry or just plain exhausted (choose the ones without added sugar)

❀ Cooled boiled water

Don't give

❀ Wheat-based foods such as pasta (commercial baby foods should say "gluten-free" for babies under 6 months)

❀ Lumpy or finger foods

❀ Salt (his kidneys can't handle it at this age)

❀ Sugar (to keep him from developing a sweet tooth)

❀ Fried foods (he needs extra fat, but not this kind)

❀ Milk, other than formula or breast

With luck, LT will take to solids like a duck to water. Most babies move on to solids without too much trouble (but a lot of mess) and then go on to enjoy meals with the family. He's bound to turn up his nose at some foods—don't worry, it won't matter if he doesn't eat some things.

How much should you give?

At first, 1 to 2 teaspoons—mix food with cooled boiled water, breast milk or formula. Give him more if he wants it. Babies know how much they need, as long as you don't tempt them with sweet foods.

If you can handle LT in a relaxed, sensitive way when he refuses food, he's less likely to develop more serious eating problems (see page 94). Ironically, many parents who worry about their babies not eating enough have overweight babies!

More of the same

Pretty soon, you'll get the hang of weaning and the chaos and

Beware right hooks!

mess involved. The bad news is, it usually gets worse before it gets better. As LT gets older, he might want to take charge of getting the food into his mouth! Good luck and don't forget to duck.

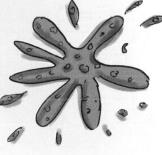

Between 4 and 6 months, LT will gradually get more and more nourishment from solids and drink less and less milk.

However, he'll still get most of his nourishment from milk until he's well over 6 months.

SUMMARY

1 Equipment: Sterilize spoons and bowls; wash bibs, blender and highchair.

2 Start between 4 and 6 months by giving him a little warm food after his milk feeding.

3 Don't force food on him or worry about the mess.

④ **Starter foods:** fruit and vegetable purées and gluten-free cereals, plus breast or formula milk.

⑤ **Memorize the "don't give" foods** on pages 25-26.

SURVIVAL TIPS

❋ **Be prepared.** He might want more than you think he will.

❋ **Instant foods are useful.** Use either commercial brands (sugar-free) or your own from the ice-cube tray, warmed up.

❀ **Keep the cupboards stocked.** Always have bananas and rice cereal handy, for example.

❀ **Stay calm** if he rejects your lovingly prepared food.

STAGE 2

ABOUT 6 TO 9 MONTHS

During this time, LT's diet will change from mostly milk to mostly solids, from puréed to mashed and then to cut-up food.

He'll be using his tongue and jaw more—vital for speech development.

Encourage him to "help" you with feeding by giving him a spoon (this is good for his hand-mouth coordination—but not your wallpaper).

Start giving him finger foods—he'll love feeding himself!

Try soft foods at first, like melon, a slice of peeled apple, peach or other fruit, or a crust of bread. Then go on to rice cakes, bread sticks or crusts of toasted bread.

He'll enjoy trying to chew, even if he doesn't have teeth yet, and it will help with teething. Always stay with Little Terror when he's eating, just in case he chokes.

What to do if LT chokes

Gently open his mouth, look inside and check for any object with your little finger. If you can't remove it or if he can't breathe, call 911 right away.

Teeth

At about 6 months, most babies start getting teeth, although this varies a great deal. Some babies are born with teeth, while others still don't have any teeth at 12 months. Most LTs should have all 20 teeth by about 18 months.

As soon as he can sit up on his own (usually about 6 months), you can feed him in his highchair. He'll love being at your height so you can look at each other and have some serious conversations! Make sure he's securely strapped in, because if you leave him for a second, he could wriggle out.

If you want to change from breast- to bottle-feeding at this point, read the manufacturer's instructions on how to make formula milk. Never increase the recommended strength. (See page 60 if you want to go right from breast to cup.)

It's a good idea to get someone else to give LT his first few bottles or he'll smell your milk and expect to be breastfed. To prevent engorged and painful breasts, reduce breastfeeding gradually by one feeding a day.

Don't let LT's lack of table manners get to you. More often than not, he'll probably spit out what you've carefully cooked for him. Stay cool and keep giving him lots of different foods (sticking to the "Dos" and "Don'ts" on pages 50-53).

Do give

❊ Same foods as first stage, but finely chopped or mashed rather than puréed

❊ Suitable family foods, such as meat, fish, chicken, and beans—remove LT's portion before adding salt or strong spices

❊ Finger foods

✻ Hard-boiled eggs and well-cooked omelettes (try tiny pieces as finger food)

✻ Gluten-containing (wheat and oat) cereals, bread and pasta

✻ Different dairy foods: add cheese to sauces, pasta, potatoes and vegetables; cottage cheese and yogurt are fine on their own or with other foods

Don't give

❊ Puréed or commercial baby foods exclusively—LT needs to get ready for chewing by working on minced and lumpy foods. Commercial baby foods can get him hooked on a special taste and he might not want to try family foods.

❊ Sweet rolls, donuts, and the like

❊ Never add sugar to cereals and drinks, or he'll develop a sweet tooth.

❋ Cow's milk, as the main milk drink—it's OK to mix it with cereals, but never use milk with reduced fat.

❋ Anything with bones that might cause LT to choke.

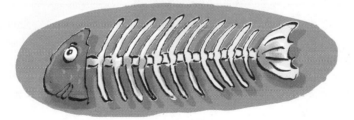

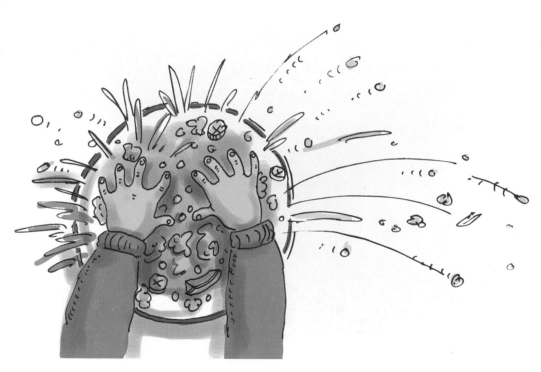

Good Feeding Guide

SUMMARY

1 **Build up to giving family foods** at each meal. Gradually reduce formula or breast milk. If he's eating a lot of solids and drinking a lot of milk, it's like having steak and potatoes followed by steak and potatoes!

2 **Don't forget finger foods.**

SURVIVAL TIPS

1. **Be prepared** for still more mess.

2. **Don't spend hours preparing something special just for LT.** Simply adapt what you're having.

3. **Keep commercial baby foods handy,** but only those without added sugar.

4. **Remember all babies are different:** Follow his pace.

⑤ **After 6 months, start cutting up his food** rather than mincing it, because he'll be starting to chew.

⑥ **Let him help himself with both hands.**

⑦ **Don't rush the meal.**

STAGE 3

9 TO 12 MONTHS

At last, Little Terror can be part of the family meals! Encourage him to chew by giving him chopped-up food rather than puréed or minced. Make it a sociable, fun time.

WAAAAH!

Making mealtimes fun

❀ Give LT a spoon or cup so he feels involved.

❀ Serve him small portions, with different shapes and colors.

❀ Give him yogurt and a spoon (but wear a raincoat!).

❀ Talk with him and show interest.

❀ Praise good behavior, ignore bad—or LT will quickly learn to manipulate mealtimes.

Bye-bye breast, hello cup

Sooner or later, you'll want to wean him from the breast or bottle to a cup. You might feel a little guilty or cruel, but you're helping LT through his next stage of development.

Exactly when you *decide to stop* breastfeeding is your choice, but keep in mind that it will be much easier at 6 months than at 2 years. A time will

Good Feeding Guide

probably come when you just feel enough is enough. Some women stop early, while others keep going until LT is getting ready for school at 3 or 4. As long as you and LT are happy, your choice will be the right one.

After 9 months, there's no point in weaning LT from breast to bottle because he needs to come off the bottle soon anyway. (Guzzling milk or juice from a bottle causes tooth decay in children over 1 year old.) Just go straight from the breast to a small cup. If you plan to give LT fruit juice, make sure it's natural and very diluted, never sweetened. The best thing to start with, however, is plain old water.

Learning to use the cup

Any time after 5 months, offer formula milk or cooled boiled water once a day from a small cup (there are some great, almost spill-proof, ones available, such as the weighted cups with two handles). Try this after lunch, when he's likely to be thirsty. If he refuses the cup, try giving him milk or water from a spoon. If he's still breastfed, get Dad or a friend to do it, so he doesn't smell your breast milk.

LT won't be happy about giving up that bedtime bottle or breast, so expect protests! Try gradually shorter feedings and then start giving him a milky drink in his cup, and lots of hugs.

Stopping the night feeding

LTs who are older than 6 months don't really need a midnight feeding and it's about time you got a decent night's sleep. If bottle-feeding, the trick is to dilute the milk gradually until it's all water, hoping LT decides it's not worth waking up

He's trying to kick the breast milk

for (see our book *The Good Sleeping Guide* for more details). If you're still breastfeeding, stop feeding him from, say, 12 a.m. to 2 a.m. and gradually increase this "no feeding" time. If necessary, get Dad to soothe LT so he doesn't smell your breast milk.

SURVIVAL TIPS

1. **Share at least one family meal a day.**
2. **Set a date for stopping breast- or bottle-feeding.** Stop bottle-feeding your LT by 1 year to avoid tooth decay.

3 **If you want to stop breastfeeding,** wear a long shirt with a high collar and no buttons. Beware loose nighties!

Good Feeding Guide

GUIDE TO HEALTHY EATING

A healthful diet from the start will benefit LT for years to come. Unlike adults and children over 5, your baby needs a lot of calories and fat in his diet to help him grow and develop. However, when he is between 2 and 3 years old, you can gradually start changing his food so that, by the time he's 5, he's on a lower-fat, higher-fiber diet. (And if your diet isn't the best, here's your chance to develop healthier habits along with LT. Why not join him and enjoy the benefit yourselves?)

Basic facts about nutrition

Calories: The body gets its fuel (or calories) in the form of protein, fat, carbohydrates, starch or sugars.

Each individual requires different amounts of fuel. LT might be highly efficient at storing energy and need fewer calories, or he could burn energy quickly and need more.

Proteins. The body manufactures protein from the carbohydrates, fats and proteins we eat. It  replaces worn-out cells and helps us grow. A newborn baby needs five times as much protein as an adult and gets this from breast or formula milk. Too much protein is stored as body fat.

Carbohydrates. The body makes carbohydrates from starches, fiber and sugars and uses them to make energy.

Starches.

Starches are three-quarters water, so they fill up LT without giving him many calories. They also contain essential vitamins and minerals. Starchy foods include potatoes, cereals and breads.

Fiber. High in bulk and nutrients and low in calories, fiber also helps prevent constipation. Children under 2 should eat very little, especially during weaning, as part of a balanced diet. Foods with fiber include bananas, carrots, apples and brown bread.

Sugars (two kinds). Unhealthful refined sugars found in candies, ice cream and white sugar provide tons of calories  but no nutrients. Natural sugars— still satisfying but less concentrated—are found in fruits and vegetables.

Fats. Fats contain vitamins, but also they have twice as many calories as protein or carbohydrates. Too much fat can make LT overweight. Foods to avoid are fatty meats, fried foods, most packaged snack foods and cakes.

Good fats are found in dairy foods, oily
fish and avocados. You can start to reduce
the fat content of LT's food after the age
of 2, but remember he needs whole milk
until he is 5.

Vitamins and minerals. Your doctor may recommend vitamin supplements (containing vitamins A, C and D) for breast-fed babies from 6 months and for bottle-fed babies if they don't drink a lot. Check with your healthcare practitioner.

The following chart lists the 5 basic food groups and the daily servings required. Keep in mind that a serving size is not large.

Food type	Examples	Daily servings
Starch	Bread, potatoes, cereal, pasta	3
Protein	Beans, poultry, nuts, meat, fish, eggs	1-2
Dairy	Milk, cheese, yogurt	2-3
Fruits	All kinds	2-4
Vegetables	All kinds, cooked and raw	3-5

Vitamin	What it does	Where you find it
A and B	Help new cells grow and release energy from carbohydrates and proteins	Milk, eggs, bread
C	Helps the body to absorb iron	All fruits and vegetables (raw is best)
D	Provides calcium for bones, heart and nerves	Sunlight, oily fish (such as sardines) and fortified baby foods
E	Strengthens cell membranes	Eggs
K	Helps blood to clot	Vegetables

 Mineral	What it does	Where you find it
Calcium	Builds bones and helps blood to clot	Dairy products and green vegetables
Fluoride	Good for bones and tooth enamel	Tap water, some teas, and some toothpastes and mouthwashes
Iron	Essential for healthy blood and normal growth and development (LT is born with a store of it, but uses it up before 6 months.)	Beans and all legume seeds, leafy vegetables, meat, eggs, prunes and other dried fruits, molasses, cocoa
Salt	Can lead to dehydration in babies and high blood pressure in adults	Many processed foods (Don't cook with salt, or add it to food.)

Snacks

Most LTs will need snacks between their three main meals. Avoid chocolate bars and choose healthful snacks, such as fresh fruit, rice cakes, raw carrots or dried apricots.

I's bound to get hungry between meals

Drinks

Milk will be LT's main drink the first year. You will also need to give water to bottle-fed babies from birth and to breastfed babies after you introduce solids. You can vary this with fruit juice diluted with water (1 part to 5 parts) at mealtimes. Sweet drinks are high in calories and bad for his teeth—avoid them.

DEVELOPING GOOD HABITS

1. Wide range of foods
2. Sensible snacks
3. Drinks: milk or water

Vegetarian diet

If you're vegetarians, you might want LT to be one too. If so, he'll grow up to be just as healthy and strong as his meat-eating friends. Follow the advice on weaning (page 12), and keep his diet varied to provide all the nutrients for good health.

Food allergies

Some babies have an allergic reaction to foods like citrus fruits, eggs, wheat cereals, nuts (which, in any case, should be finely ground to prevent choking) and peanut butter. If you have a family history of asthma or eczema, or an allergy to nuts, LT could inherit the same problems.

Don't introduce these foods until he's at least 6 months old, and then only in small amounts and one at a time, so that you can watch his reaction closely. There is strong evidence that breastfeeding, and waiting until LT is 5 months old before introducing solids, can offer some protection.

Allergic reaction to nuts can be severe. Look for tummy pain, difficulty breathing, pale complexion and clammy skin. If you suspect a reaction, call 911 immediately. He'll need an injection, followed by a careful diet, avoiding peanuts and their oils in particular.

WEANING PROBLEMS

CHECK LIST

1 Refusing solids? Check with your doctor. LT might not be physically ready for solids. Try again in a week or two, but don't make it a fight. Breast- or bottle-feed him first, because he's still learning, then a try a tiny amount of solids.

2 **Are you staying calm?** If you get irritated when LT clamps his mouth shut or spits out everything, LT will soon learn he gets your attention by not eating. Try to keep calm. He isn't really objecting to solids— he just prefers the milk. Given the choice, most babies do.

Stay relaxed

③ **Still wants lots of milk?** Feeding on demand is fine at 6 weeks but not so good at 12 months. Long before 6 months, a baby can fill up on milk within a few minutes, so he may have trouble telling the difference between food and comfort. Think of milk as a meal. After 6 months he needs solids; if he fills up on milk, he won't have room for them.

④ **Refusing milk?** He's not doing it just to bug you. Some babies refuse milk after you stop breast- or bottle-feeding. If he's gaining weight and wetting his diaper, don't worry. To make sure he gets enough vitamin D, try giving him milk in other forms,

Good Feeding Guide

such as yogurt or cheese. If he likes solids, he should get plenty of nutrients. Check with your healthcare practitioner if you're worried.

⑤ **Overeating?** He might not know when he's had enough. Remember that if you're giving LT milk *plus* a full meal, he's going through the entire menu twice. As he moves on to solids, replace some of the milk with water at each feeding. If LT is on solids and looking chubby, turn to the healthful-eating section and make sure he's getting his calories from carbohydrates, not fats and sugars.

If you give LT foods that contain refined sugars, he will overeat

6 **Undereating?** Keep in mind he'll gain twice as much weight in his first six months as in his second six months. His appetite may seem to slow down by the time he starts eating solids. He may not be as thin as you think. What shape are you? He might be growing in length

Weight gain will probably slow down as crawling speeds up

Good Feeding Guide

rather than width. Check with your healthcare practitioner. If he's not too active yet, he'll need less food than a baby who's moving all over the place.

☑ **Refusing food?** Could he simply have an independent streak and want to feed himself? Don't fall into the trap of resorting to snacks instead of healthful food just to get something inside him.

DEVELOPING GOOD HABITS

1 Make eating fun. Try to be patient if LT takes his own sweet time. Look at him and chat. Eat with him or brush up on your acting and pretend to.

2 Get into a routine. Do this as soon as you can, so that LT learns what a mealtime is.

③ Weaning Tips

❈ Don't force solids.

❈ Don't reward him with extra attention for not eating.

❈ He can survive without milk, but give him substitutes.

❈ LT is not always the best judge of how much is enough.

EATING PROBLEMS

If he doesn't have serious health problems and isn't affected by any family problems, Little Terror can overcome most eating difficulties if you handle him in the right way. Problems come in all shapes and sizes. Perhaps LT barely eats at all, or eats all the wrong foods. He might want to eat at the wrong times (midnight, for example), or maybe he never sits down to eat. Does it seem like Little Terror is calling all the shots?

It's easy to feel hopeless. But you do have helpful options. Use the checklist below to get a clear picture of his eating habits. Then read the survival tips that follow to see what you can do about it.

CHECK LIST

LT doesn't eat much

☑ **Is it really a problem?** Is he growing OK according to the percentile chart at your doctor's office?

2 **Are you rewarding him with lots of attention** when he doesn't eat?

3 **What and when does he eat,** and who eats with him?

Won't sit down to eat

1 Are you expecting LT to sit still too long?

Are your expectations
realistic?

② Is it time for LT to stop using the high chair?

SURVIVAL TIPS

If LT doesn't eat much or just picks at his food

1 **Never force him to eat.** Just take away the food after about a half-hour. You'll know that he's probably had enough when he pushes the bowl of food onto the floor, turns his head away when you try to give

him that extra spoonful, or
refuses to swallow what he
has in his mouth.

2 **Make sure he's not overtired.**
A sleepy
child rarely
has an
appetite.

Is he
overtired?

3 Give him lots of praise when he eats just a little more than he did before. Try to ignore his non-eating games.

Good Feeding Guide

4 **Share regular meals** so that he has company, sees you eating, maybe even tries something off your plate. Invite his friend who eats like a horse to lunch. Relatives or friends eating with you take the pressure and attention off LT, and he might eat without anyone noticing.

If LT eats the wrong food: snacks and sweets

① He's not going to feel hungry for a healthful meal if he's snacking all the time. See the Guide to Healthy Eating on page 69.

② Give him small portions to start with.

For example, just two peas, a quarter of a baked potato, and a little grated cheese.

③ **Make it fun.** Let LT choose a special plastic plate and bowl at the store, and let him get it out himself before mealtimes.

④ **Are there other problems to solve** before you tackle the eating problems? Ask your healthcare practitioner for advice.

Make it fun

5 **Tell Grandma and Mrs. Knowitall** that it's nice of them to give him pieces of their cinnamon rolls, but you're having a hard time with meals at the moment, so would they please keep treats to themselves for a while!

⑥ **LT might seem to be eating nothing,** but if you add up all the snacks, you may find a ton of calories without much nutrition.

Is he sitting comfortably?

1️⃣ **Don't let him run around during mealtimes.** Make it a social time. Eat with him.

2️⃣ **Give lots of praise for good behavior.**

3️⃣ **Bad behavior?** Ignore it, if possible.

④ **Be prepared.** If he's hungry and has to wait, he might lose interest. He won't sit still for long.

⑤ **Is the TV on?** It will distract him from eating.

Sweets

Candy and cookies are OK, but dried fruit is better—in moderation. Let him choose one treat from the cookie jar or candy dish after lunch each day and then clean his teeth. Never let him push you into giving him more. Children adapt more quickly than you think. He'll start to eat his lunch, knowing he'll be rewarded.

Snacks

If he has an eating problem, don't allow snacks. If he fills up on crackers, he won't have an appetite for healthful food.

If you're patient, Little Terror will happily ease into solids. We hope you now have some idea of how to resolve any problems you come across. Forming healthy eating habits now will give LT a great start in life. Keep experimenting with new tastes, colors and textures, and you'll be opening him up to one of life's greatest pleasures—good food.

Eating Problems

INDEX

NOTES:

Good Feeding Guide

Notes:

NOTES:

Good Feeding Guide